Driving

by **Dana Meachen Rau**

Reading Consultant: Nanci R. Vargus, Ed. D.

Marshall Cavendish
Benchmark
New York

Picture Words

bus

car

cars

city

dump truck

farmer's

field

fire engine

kids

motorcycle

race cars

road

taxi

tractor

Vrooom!

The 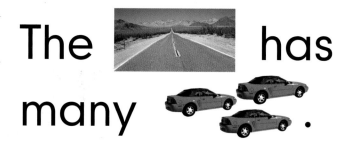 has many .

A  drives to school.

A  drives
to a fire.

A  drives through a .

drive fast around a track.

A  drives on a long .

A  drives in a 🧑‍🌾's .

A  drives on a dirt .

A  takes you where you want to go.

Vrooooom!

Words to Know

fast   to move quickly

road   (rohd)
a path from one place to
another

school (skool)
a place where children learn

Find Out More

Books

Bridges, Sarah. *I Drive a Dump Truck*. Minneapolis, MN: Picture Window Books, 2005.

Hill, Lee Sullivan. *Motorcycles*. Minneapolis, MN: Lerner Publications, 2004.

Owen, Ann. *Taking You Places: A Book about Bus Drivers*. Minneapolis, MN: Picture Window Books, 2005.

Walker, Pamela. *Welcome Books: Car Rides*. Danbury, CT: Children's Press, 2000.

Videos

Daignault, Robert A. *Hard Hat Harry's Trucks and Fire Trucks*. Good Times, 2005.

Hood, David. *There Goes a Motorcycle*. Kid Vision.

Web Sites

How Stuff Works: Fire Engines
http://people.howstuffworks.com/fire-engine.htm

Peterson Automotive Museum
http://www.petersen.org/

Wheels Through Time: The Museum that Runs
http://www.wheelsthroughtime.com/

About the Author

Dana Meachen Rau is an author, editor, and illustrator. A graduate of Trinity College in Hartford, Connecticut, she has written more than one hundred books for children, including nonfiction, biographies, early readers, and historical fiction. She drives all around her town of Burlington, Connecticut.

About the Reading Consultant

Nanci R. Vargus, Ed.D, wants all children to enjoy reading. She used to teach first grade. Now she works at the University of Indianapolis. Nanci helps young people become teachers. She often drives to Cincinnati to see her granddaughters, Charlotte and Corinne.

Marshall Cavendish Benchmark
99 White Plains Road
Tarrytown, NY 10591-9001
www.marshallcavendish.us

All Internet sites were correct at time of printing.

Library of Congress Cataloging-in-Publication Data

Rau, Dana Meachen, 1971–
Driving / by Dan Meachen Rau
     p. cm. — (Benchmark rebus)
Summary: "Easy to read text with rebuses explores various vehicles"—Provided by publisher.
Includes bibliographical references.
ISBN-13: 978-0-7614-2316-4
ISBN-10: 0-7614-2316-8
Motor vehicles—Juvenile literature. 2. Motor vehicle driving—Juvenile literature. 3. Rebuses—Juvenile literature.
I. Title. II. Series: Rau, Dana Meachen, 1971– . Benchmark rebus.

Editor: Christine Florie
Editorial Director: Michelle Bisson
Art Director: Anahid Hamparian
Series Designer: Virginia Pope

Photo research by Connie Gardner

Rebus images, with the exception of the farmer, provided courtesy of *Dorling Kindersley*.

Cover photo by Peter M. Fisher/*Corbis*

The photographs in this book are used with permission and through the courtesy of:
Corbis: p. 2 farmer, Royalty Free; p. 5 Royalty Free; p. 9 Patrick Bennett; p. 11 Royalty Free; p. 15 Tim Pannell;
p. 19 Raymond Gehman; *Photo Researchers*: p. 7 Richard Hutchings; *The Image Works*: p. 13 Michael Okoniewski;
p. 17 Joe Sohm; *SuperStock*: p. 21 Digital Vision Ltd.

Printed in Malaysia
1 3 5 6 4 2